*For Ethan and Dana, as we pray together – J.B.*

*For Mali – L.F.*

### *Acknowledgements*

page 6: Traditional. Page 7: Anonymous. Page 8: Edith Rutter Leatham (1870-1939). Page 9: Traditional. Pages 10-11: 1st verse traditional, 2nd verse © Jeremy Brooks. Page 12: 18th-century German hymn translated into English as 'We Plough the Fields and Scatter'. Page 13: Traditional Cherokee blessing. Page 14: From *The Prayer Garden: An Anthology of Children's Prayers*, Christopher Herbert, Bishop of St Albans. Page 15: 'A Child's Prayer' from *Children's Prayers from Around the World*, ed. Mary Batchelor (Lion, 1977). Page 16: Traditional. Page 17: Paramahansa Yogananda, founder of Self-Realisation Fellowship (1893-1952). Pages 18-19: Victor Hugo (1802-85). Page 20: © The United Educators, Inc. Page 21: English translation, from the opera *Hänsel und Gretel*, Engelbert Humperdinck (1854-1921). The publishers apologise to any copyright holders they were unable to trace and would like to hear from them.

First published in Great Britain in 2008 and the USA in 2009 by
Frances Lincoln Children's Books, 4 Torriano Mews,
Torriano Avenue, London NW5 2RZ
www.franceslincoln.com

British Library Cataloguing in Publication Data
available on request

ISBN: 978-1-84507-535-4

Illustrated with watercolours, acrylics and pencil

Set in Stone Informal

Printed in Singapore
9 8 7 6 5 4 3 2 1

# My First Prayers

Selected by The Reverend Jeremy Brooks

Illustrated by Laure Fournier

FRANCES LINCOLN
CHILDREN'S BOOKS

O God, my Father, stay always with me.
In the morning, in the evening,
by day or by night, always be my helper.

*Poland*

Keep my little tongue today,
keep it gentle while I play.
Keep my hands from doing wrong,
keep my feet the whole day long.
Keep me all, O Jesus mild,
keep me ever thy dear child.

*USA*

Heaven

6

7

3

5

2

4

1

Thank you for the world so sweet,
thank you for the food we eat,
thank you for the birds that sing –
thank you, God, for everything.

*England*

God is great, God is good,
let us thank him for our food.

*USA*

Dear Jesus, bless my hands today,
and may the things they do
be kind and loving, strong and good,
two busy hands for you.

Dear Jesus, bless my every deed
and guide each word I say.
Help me, Lord, to work for you
and do my best today.

*England*

All good gifts around us
are sent from heaven above.
Then thank the Lord,
O thank the Lord
for all his love.

*Germany*

May the warm winds of heaven
blow softly upon your house.
May the Great Spirit
bless all who enter there.
May your moccasins
make happy tracks in many snows,
and may the rainbow
always touch your shoulder.

*Native America*

For buckets and spades, for sunshine and shade,
for sand in the toes, for cream on the nose,
for jumping the tide, for having a ride,
for laughter and fun, praise God, everyone.

*England*

Thank God for rain
and the beautiful rainbow colours,
and thank God for letting children
splash in the puddles.

*England*

O God, look on us and be always with us,
that we may live happily.

*South Africa*

Naughty or good, I am your child.

*India*

Good night! Good night!
Far flies the light,
but still God's love
shall flame above,
making all bright.
Good night! Good night!

*France*

Sleep my little one!
The night is all wind and rain;
The meal has been wet
by the raindrops
and bent is the sugar cane;
O Giver who gives to the people,
in safety my little son keep!
My little son with the head-dress,
sleep, sleep, sleep!

*East Africa*

When at night I go to sleep
fourteen angels watch do keep.
Two my head are guarding,
two my feet are guiding,
two are on my right hand,
two are on my left hand,
two who warmly cover,
two who o'er me hover,
two to whom is given
to guide my steps to Heaven.

*Germany*